Basic Research Guide (BaReGu)

Anna C. Bocar
Author

DEDICATION

I would like to express my deepest gratitude for the support extended by my husband Manolo who unselfishly provided me a quiet space to write this booklet, my daughter Analou who untiringly showed inspiration to continue writing on despite all difficulties I encountered, my son Manolo Ivy who willingly gave his sweet smiles when I was almost to give up. In addition, to my late daughter Ivy, who continuously lighten my biggest challenges in writing this booklet.

My gracious appreciation to my colleagues and friends who thoughtfully demonstrated their gestures of concern and encouragement, Noeme, Prudelen, Carousel and especially Marylene and Dr. Elsie L. Dajao who gave time to read and edit this compilation and advised re-writing of some statements for clarity.

CONTENTS

Basic Research Guide

PREFACE

What has gone astray to the efficiency of some researchers is the knowledge on how to conduct the research. Familiarity or awareness on other relevant points that need to be kept in mind to achieve better output is likewise significant. Constant practice of the skills that each researcher possesses will lead him or her to become a better researcher.

This material is rigorously compiled to provide a guiding tool to be utilized by the researchers especially the students. Though most of the sources of this paper come from online articles, this is accomplished through excessive and extensive hard work of study.

Moreover, this compilation aims to lighten the burden of those who feel that research is extremely a difficult task to do. It is also hoped that with this material, research paper writing may become easier to students as this shows simpler, clearer and more understandable guidelines and steps. Having the basic knowledge on how to conduct and write a research paper will make it a lot easier and more fun. One will be able to produce not only an educative paper but also a scholarly academic document.

BASIC GUIDE I

Brief Guidelines

The topic about research for the majority is an issue to be thought about. It seems they consider it a burden and hard to do. Research work is not as difficult as what others think. As it is defined, research is a purposeful, precise and systematic search for new knowledge, skills, attitudes and values, or for the re-interpretation of existing knowledge, abilities, behaviors and values ("Research Methods", n.d.). Researchers' task is to make use of the existing data to find results whether this fact is also true to other environment.

In doing a research study, the researchers must be cautious. They must allocate plenty of time to complete each activity. They must be conscientious and they must work in the library for a certain number of hours each week. They need to add some more weeks before the scheduled deadline because there are some things that take more time than what is planned, and there are some stages in research work that are more difficult than what they expect. In short, there are unexpected difficulties and problems that may lead to academic failures (Trimmer, 1992). Moreover, research work requires time. It is rewarding when the goal to finish it is attained on the target date. Thus, a researcher needs to manage time properly.

Basic Research Guide

Indeed, research work is a tedious, tiring and a very laborious task to accomplish. Most often, this is an academic requirement that teachers and students cannot get rid from doing. They must therefore have the interest of doing it.

Since students are neophyte researchers, the teacher must give them specific instructions and guide them step by step. On the same manner, the students must follow the steps and must be cautious with the time allotted for each step. They must be prompt in passing their first draft; they must be guided and must apply all the corrections and suggestions their teacher gave upon submission of their final paper.

In conducting a study, the researcher must have the positive answer to the following questions:

- What is the topic or issue you like to study?
- What makes it interesting?
- Why do you like to know about this topic or issue?
- What contribution could your study give to the society?
- What are the principles, theories, and/or models that challenge you to conduct your study?
- How are you going to conduct your research?
- Are the respondents of your study reachable?
- Can you approach your respondents without hesitations?

- What statistical methods are you going to use in the interpretation of your study?

Attitudes Researchers Should Possess

College students must set their minds that in their tertiary level they will undertake various researches. Writing a research is a multi-tasking work that takes a long process and it is coupled with editing, and adhering to very strict deadlines. All primary/secondary sources must be properly cited. To be prepared they must have to possess: (1) a "can do," positive attitude. – means the readiness to do the research and the belief that it is doable; (2) mental willingness to do the project - means the interest to conduct the research must be present ; (3) intellectual skill – means the strong fundamental knowledge on how to write a research paper has been established ("Writing Policy", 2009).

Thirteen Good Personal Qualities of a Researcher

A good researcher must possess necessary personal qualities to succeed in his/her endeavor for excellence. Below are the qualities that must be considered:

Diligence. Gathering the data for a research work is not an easy task. You should work hard. You must be industrious and you must work in a meticulous way.

Futuristic. Think in advance. It is necessary that you have already in your mind the answers of the primary questions in conducting a research, namely: what to do, how to do, and where to conduct the research.

Consistency. You must concentrate and must be firm. Do not deviate from the topic or issue that you have raised at the start of your study. Do not raise another topic or issue in the text of your work. It might cause some troubles and confusions. The things, acts, or statements that you use at the beginning should be in accordance to or in harmony with what had been previously done, expressed or agreed upon and must have logical connections.

Prudence. You must have to be habitually careful to avoid errors. Be cautious, and exercise sound judgment at all times. Do not allow your carelessness ruin or destroy your intense desire to finish your research work.

Broad - mindedness and Perseverance. There might be unexpected things, acts or statements that you may encounter along the way in the making of your research paper. Have a broad mind to understand the situations that may occur. Be liberal in beliefs and opinions of other people. This will strengthen the content of your study.

Determination. To have your name printed on a research paper is a great reward to your hard work. Start doing your study with great intention of finishing it. Settle your mind and decide that you must have to reach the completion of your study.

Willingness. Have and keep the flame of your interest burning. Direct yourself to the right path. Never let some unexpected circumstances to change the course of your desire to finish you research work.

Resourcefulness. Have the ability to search useful facts that will substantiate the study. Search for fertile resources and have the pool of theories relevant to the study.

Patience. Loosen your belt. Hold your temper because you, your teacher or your adviser are unique individuals. You have different viewpoints in certain situations but as a team you will have to work the research study hand in hand until the paper is finally done. Be calm. The forbearance on the faults or infirmities of others is virtue. Endure without complaint.

Passion and Endurance. Think that research work is easy. Be ready to handle difficult, unexpected situations along the way.

Basic Research Guide

Responsibility. Do the writing with the capacity of perceiving what is right or wrong.

Honesty. This is an important aspect in doing a research. Unreliable results are products of dishonesty.

Time Consciousness. Stick and strictly observe your schedule.

Two Kinds of Undergraduate Research Papers

Andres & Andres presented two kinds of undergraduate papers. These are:

> (1) report form – the writer wishes to find out the facts of his subject and present them in a clear, orderly, and detailed account,

> (2) thesis research paper - the writer studies the facts to draw a conclusion from them (p 36). Arrangement is modified.

Research and Its Definition

From the Encyclopedia of Social Science, (as cited by Estolas, & Boquirin, 1973) research is derived from the old French word "cerchier" meaning to seek or search and "re" prefix meaning

" again" signifies replication of the search. It is the manipulation of thing, concepts or symbols for the reason for summing up to expand, spot-on or check information whether that learning helps in the development of a certain principle. In brief, it is to seek or search again. Estolas, & Boquirin (1973) added another definition from the Webster's Third New International Dictionary which declares that, it is the revision of an approved end point, acknowledge by the expert in the light of newfound realities, conclusions, theories or laws. An online article entitled   Research and Writing, (n.d.) it states that:

Research is the integral element of accomplishing a superior quality assignment. It is one of the most time and effort consuming tasks involved in writing academic papers. It will require researcher to study a lot of books, journal articles and credible Internet websites.

Research Paper and Its Definition

A research paper is the final product of a process. These processes are the critical thinking, source evaluating, organizing, and composing of the gathered ideas. The sources of information linked to the topic were discovered , construed and evaluated. Hamid & Baker (2007) on their online article revealed that:

Basic Research Guide

The nourishment of a research paper comes from the primary and secondary; the backed-up and collaboration of the sources mentioned earlier would lead the paper to the appropriate genre of writing (e.g., an encyclopedic article). Research paper serves not only to further the field in which it is written, but also to offer the researchers with unique chance to deepen their knowledge in that field.

The student who is writing a summary of a topic, book report, an opinion piece, expository essay is not producing a research paper. This work consists solely of his/her own interpretation of a text nor an overview of a particular topic. The goal of a research is to draw on what others have to say about a topic. Research is exploring and assessing the sources with intent to offer an interpretation of the gathered data.

Research Paper Writing

For many students, to be given a research paper assignment sounds to be intimidating and stressful. One needs to be familiar on how to write a research paper. He/she must have to be sure on what is the course of action in writing and what would be the content of his/her paper. Those who are familiar on how to write a research paper find it easy; thus, the researcher must be familiar with an academic research because a research paper includes significant research. Before he or she can successfully finish a research paper he/she must know how to find, assess and comment scholarly research. There are steps to be followed so that the research paper assignment can be completed in due time. These steps are: (1) carefully note those statements which you think have the relevance to your assignment while doing the research, (2) assemble an outline; and (3) write the draft (Moore, 1999).

A student should know other significant skills in writing a research paper. These are: (1) How to write research paper notes. Research paper notes are different from the type of notes a student will take in class. It must be very detailed. The use of quotations and citations must be done properly and carefully. (2) How to write research paper outlines. The research notes must be incorporated into the outline. After composing an outline, a student needs only to follow the outline to create the research paper draft ("How to Write Research Paper", n.d.).

Research Proposal Writing

Most if not all graduate degrees require the students to submit a research output and before a researcher could have an output a research proposal is to be submitted first to a committee.

Accordingly, a proposal must indicate what, how and where it will be done and that results are looked forward to. From the beginning all of these things must be clarified. When some matters relating to research proposal are unclear to the researcher this will lead to fruitless thesis writing.

Upon approval of the research proposal, the committee will give their best judgment and as such, they impliedly agree that the results after the study is conducted will be regarded as sufficient for granting a degree. After writing the proposal, the researcher has visualized or anticipated already the possible results to happen in the course of the study. The proponent must have in mind a good idea and such will come from some acquaintances of the topic. To possess good idea on the topic to be researched the proponent must have good foundation through reading some materials related to the topic. This does not mean only reading, but also through some observing and discussing such topic.

In writing the proposal, one must read everything that he/she believes linkable to the topic of interest. The important and missing part of such topic must be outlined. To load the missing part of it is the important part in a research. It is where the researcher will know more about it. The questions stocked in his/her mind will be given enlightenment. The proposal will help the proponent to foresee the range of the project. The project must not be too big. Five to ten pages will be good enough in a proposal. The proponent needs to give an idea about how the project is to be conducted and what difference will the output bring.

The questions that the research needs to answer must be specified; set up why they are important questions, show how they answered the questions are answered, and point out who will be benefited in the output of this project. The proposal should be anchored to some theories or related literature. It must be persuasive to the committee that the way it is to be done will give reasonable answer to the questions (Mc Granaghan, n.d.).

Research Outline and Its Importance

"Creating an outline before writing your research paper will make organizing your thoughts a lot easier. Making any kind of outline will be beneficial to your writing process" ("Why and How to Create a Useful Outline", 2007).

Thesis Format Guidelines

The development in research paper writing can be achieved by means of excellent preparation, strict record keeping, and practice ("Informal Guidelines", 2010). In submitting a manuscript the

following should be considered:

1. Page Size: 8.5" X 11"
    1.1 Left Margin: 1.5"

Basic Research Guide

1.2 Right Margin: 1"
1.3 Top Margin: 1"
1.4 Bottom Margin: 1"

2. Font type of all text should be Times New Roman.
3. Paper Title should be of Font Size 14, center text
4. Author 's Name in Font Size of 14, center text
5. "ABSTRACT" Font size of 12 Bold.
6. Main Text: Font size 12 with justified columns section (except sentences in the tables)

Tables:
Table number and title is positioned above the table
Table number should be non-italics;

Table title should be italicized

All Major Words in *Table Title* should be capitalized. No full stop (.) at end of name

Table headers should be bolded and the first letter should be capitalized.

All table content should be single spaced and should be left- aligned except numbers which should be typed   at the center

Only two decimal points should show
in numbers (generally)

(leave 1 double line spaces between the table
and following text)
Figures:
Leave   1 double line space
from the above   text and
figure itself

Leave 1 double line space
below the figure number
before the title of the figure is
placed
Italicized the Figure number
(example: *Figure 1)*

There must be a period after
the number (i.e. *Figure 1-1.*)

Figure title should not be
italicized.

Capitalize the proper nouns
and   first letter only of the
figure title;

7. Page numbers: font size 12

Note: Latest corrected paper must be submitted

Basic Research Guide

to the adviser / teacher together with the new copy.

Page Cover Format

(Observe correct balance; apply inverted pyramid format)

Sample:

DIFFICULTIES ENCOUNTERED BY THE STUDENT-RESEARCHERS AND THE EFFECTS ON THEIR RESEARCH OUTPUT
(Note: should **not be more than 15 words** including articles, prepositions, etc)

_____35 spaces_____

A Research Paper Presented to the Faculty of College of Arts and Sciences La Salle University – Ozamiz

_____30 spaces_____

In Partial Fulfillment of the Requirements for the Degree Bachelor of Science and Criminology

_____25 spaces_____

by
ANNA C. BOCAR
March 2019

Brief Guidelines and Outline on the Parts of a Research Paper

TITLE

- Must be revealing; short, clear and specific; should not have non-standard acronyms or abbreviations; should not exceed two printed lines; should not exceed to 15 words including articles, etc.; font size 14,centered; (" Informal Guidelines", 2010)
- all in capital letters
- if the title is more than one line continue to the next line after the other
- Leave 2 double line spaces to begin the next line

Author's name
- center text, in font size 14

APPROVAL SHEET
(leave 2 double line spaces below to begin Text: font size 12; each line single space)

ACKNOWLEDGMENT
(leave 2 double line spaces below to begin) (Text: font size 12; leave 1 double - space every after each line)

ABSTRACT
(font size of 12;   Bold letters for the word

Basic Research Guide

" ABSTRACT")

(leave 1 double line space below the word abstract to begin)

Characteristics of an abstract:

-brief distinct paragraph;   should be   300 words or less; unindented; single space; summary of the study; comprehensive sentences;   should be easily grasped;   to the point description of the research;   avoid citing references at this point; should be brief, clear, logical; should not have abnormal acronyms or abbreviations; ("Informal Guidelines", 2010)

Content of the abstract:

- reason of the study, theory, overall issue (research topic/ question) , purpose / fundamental goal; accurate statistics; relevant results;   key findings; conclusions (" Informal Guidelines", 2010)

TABLE OF CONTENTS
(leave 2 double line spaces below to begin ; should be   based on research output)

LIST OF TABLES
(leave 2 double line spaces below to begin ; should be based on research output)

LIST OF FIGURES

(leave 2 double line spaces below to begin ;
should be based on research output)

CHAPTER 1

(leave   1 double   line   space followed the title of
chapter 1)

THE PROBLEM AND ITS SCOPE

INTRODUCTION

(leave 2 double line spaces   from the last line to
begin)

Rationale of the Study (- a sort of introduction;
state the problem that needs to be addressed)
(leave 1 double   space below to begin)

Key points:
- thoughts must be arranged from
general view point of the researcher to
specific (mirror principle); employ common
terms; discuss sufficient background
information; present the basis of the study;
specifically outline the theory / purpose of
the study; describe, explain the problem in a
reasonable way visibly, logically; construct
key point with every section; reason/s that
encourage the researcher to investigate or
conduct the study (" Informal Guidelines",
2010)
(leave 2 double line spaces from last line

Basic Research Guide

to begin)

Review of Related Literature / Related Studies

(leave 1 double space below to begin)

The review of related literature format depends on the kind of discipline. This is often a section in theses and dissertations. This is a requirement in a research proposal. Literature review is a section that a published body of knowledge, prior research studies, and theoretical articles are reviewed, summarized, classified, or compared by the researcher ("APA Documentation", 2009).

Since the intention of the literature review section is to offer an impression of significant literature which are in connection to the present study, the researcher needs to do some assessment or examination of academic papers and informative materials and other sources which are essential before writing the literature review. The resources to be assessed or examined must be relevant to the present topic, particular issue, area of research or theory; a description, summary and critical evaluation of each work must be provided.

There are four important questions in constructing a literature review section: (1) What is the research topic and what issues are included in the topic?; (2) Can sources that are relevant to the topic investigated be found?; (3) Can the sources at hand when put together contribute greater understanding to the present topic?; (4) Are these scholarly articles applicable to the present study? ("Write a Literature Review", 2011).

(leave 2 double line spaces from last line to begin)

Theoretical Background (Framework) / Conceptual Framework
(leave 1 double line space below to begin; brief introduction of this section is needed)

This section provides the theories, principles, philosophy, premise, foundation, basis , or groundwork which the proposed study is

anchored on. This also imparts conceptual basics upon which an issue is based (Salier, 2008).

This part introduces a summary, synthesis of principles, theories in which the study is anchored on that can be used to support Chapter 3; recommendations from other researchers of similar study; take notice : consult your statement of the problem and questionnaire

(leave 2 double line spaces from last line to begin)

Statement of the Problem
(leave 1 double line space below to begin; short introduction is needed in this section)

Basic Research Guide

This section would be in a question form; state the general problem, then specifically enumerate the question/s that need to be addressed or answered.

(leave 2 double line spaces from last line to begin)

Significance of the Study
(leave 1 double- space below to begin; introduction for this section is needed)

This segment of the research paper will tell the reader who will be benefited on the results of the study.

CHAPTER 2
(leave 1 double line space below for title of chapter 2 to follow)

METHOD
(leave 2 double line spaces   to begin; a short introduction of this section is needed   )

Design
(leave 1 double line space below to begin)

This part presents the research method used in the study.

(leave 2 double line spaces from last line to begin)

Environment / Locale / Setting / Location

(leave 1 double line space below to begin)

This section presents the description of the environment; the setting or place where the research is conducted.

(leave 2 double line spaces from last line to begin)

Respondents
(leave 1 double line   space below to begin)

This part describes specifically the respondents of the study.

(leave 2 double line spaces from last line to begin)

Instruments Used   (tool in gathering the data)
(leave 1 double line space below to begin)

This part supplies information to the reader on what tool is utilized in gathering the data of the study. The tool could be an adopted, standard survey questionnaire; a modified questionnaire from the original; or a self-devised or constructed questionnaire.

(leave 2 double line spaces from last line to begin)

Data Gathering Procedure
(leave 1 double line space below to begin)

This section explains the course of actions /

Basic Research Guide

approaches / procedures / processes / methods / techniques / manners / mode or way on how the data are gathered.

(leave 2 double line spaces from last line to begin)

Statistical Tool / Treatment of Data
(leave 1 double line space below to begin)

This part introduces the statistical method used to interpret the gathered data (ex. ANOVA, chi-square, weighted mean, frequency distribution, percentile and the like).

CHAPTER 3
(leave 1 single line space below followed by title of chapter 3)

PRESENTATION, ANALYSIS AND INTERPRETATION OF DATA

- a short introduction is needed before discussion of the results begins

(leave 1 double line space to begin)

This is a research - based section. The gathered data should be arranged correctly and accurately. Each table presented in the study must have an interpretation based on the results of the study. The discussion should be well organized. The compiled related literature / related studies may be used to support or contrast the results of the present study.

CHAPTER 4
(leave 2 double line spaces below to begin the title of chapter 4)

SUMMARY OF FINDINGS, CONCLUSION AND RECOMMENDATIONS
(leave 1   double   line space to begin)

The brief introductory statements should be written in this part to give the readers an idea on what to expect in this section.

(leave 2 double line spaces from last line to begin)

Findings
(leave 1 double line space below to begin; opening statements   are needed)

This may be in an enumerated form or in a paragraph form. The researcher/s in this part should present the noteworthy, remarkable or significant matters observed from the results of the study other than what were presented in results and discussion section. The FINDINGS should have to answer the problems stipulated in Chapter 1, and other indispensable results found in the study must be laid down as part of this section.

Basic Research Guide

(leave 2 double line spaces from last line to begin)

Conclusion
(leave 1 double line space below to begin; laid an introductory statements)

The CONCLUSION is in a paragraph form. This part should state what the researcher found after the investigation or study was conducted.   This is the end point of the discussion. This will disclose the **"sorted-revealed fact".**
(leave 2 double line spaces from last line to begin)

Recommendation/s
(leave 1 double line space below to begin; opening statements are needed)

The RECOMMENDATION/S should be in an enumerated form. This section confers suggestion, proposition, idea, and proposal on what should be done to address the issue investigated.

References
(leave 2 double line spaces to begin)

The word "References" should be written at the center; list of references must be in alphabetical order.

In this page list every source in single line space but   observe hanging indention for the second line.

(leave 1 double line spaces every after each source)

APPENDICES
-the word "Appendices" should be written at the center of the page intended for it

      Everything in the appendix should be single spaced.

Important Note: A Chapter must start in a new page; pagination is silent; meaning a chapter page must not contain a page number;   the 13 good personal qualities a researcher should possess must be strictly observed.

BASIC GUIDE II

Research Methods

Teachers need to provide students an overview

Basic Research Guide

of research methods with emphasis on both conceptual understanding and skills which students can use in the future either in research or at work. The following are some of research methods questions and issues:

(1)   Question   Formulation.   Researcher should know about the topic for the study that he/she is going to conduct. His background could be informal-personal experiences or everything that can be picked up in life, or formal-education and training in his profession ("Research Methods", 2005).   Fact, opinion, attitude, and demographic are examples of questions to be asked in a study. Researchers should write clear, definite, answerable questions. The questionnaire should be pre-tested to assure the quality of responses (Le Gates, 1999).

(2) Topic.   Before proceeding to the research task**, ask** yourself: "Do I want to do research on this topic?" AND "Can I do the research on this topic?" The researcher's interest in the topic and the feasibility of carrying out research on the topic are the two factors that influence the choice of a research topic. In choosing the topic, the researcher should have interest on it. A topic of personal interest to the

researcher commonly leads to better quality research. The other factor to be considered is the researcher's capability to actually conduct the study; resources and access to the population are of particular importance. The scope of the topic should be set

("Research Methods", 2005).

(3) Design. There are questions that a researcher should answer ahead of time regarding the intended study to be conducted. These are:

(3.1) how will the study be conducted? This refers to the manner, method, procedure, approach to be employed in the study. Research instrument or tool for the study is to be considered;

(3.2) what will be studied? It is about the topic to be investigated;

(3.3) where will the study be conducted? This refers to the research environment. The place where the study has to take place;

(3.4) who will be studied? Refers to population and the sampling technique to be used;

(3.5) when will the study be conducted? Time allocation ("Research Methods", 2005).

(4) Sample Size. According to Hinkle (as cited in Le Gates,1999) "various approaches are available for determining the sample size needed for obtaining a specified degree of accuracy in estimation of population parameters from sample statistics. All of these methods assume 100% returns from a random sample". Le Gates argued that small populations require responses from substantial proportions of their membership to generate the same accuracy that a much smaller proportion will yield for a much larger population. For example, a random sample of 132 is required for a population of 200 to achieve the same accuracy that a random sample of 384 will provide for a population of one million. In cases such as the former, it usually makes more sense to poll the entire population than to sample.

Questionnaire Development

Almost all aim to become good researchers, if not the best with relevant research output; however, they encounter many problems, more so, if they are just beginners.

Note: To give some ideas and with the mission to help the compiler prepared the succeeding topics with the guidance of the work of Robert B. Frary (2007), the author of an on line scholarly paper entitled "A Brief Guide to Questionnaire Development". Arrangement was changed / modified to give the reader more convenience and easier way to grasp and remember.

What are the causes of unsatisfactory results of questionnaires?
These are because of the following:

- inexperienced developer
- inadequate consideration of aspects of
      questionnaire process
- questionnaire's deficiency
- respondents' little concern on the
      questions they answered

Preliminary considerations by questionnaire developer.

He/she must have:
- to possess mental discipline
      - to obtain feedback from a small but
      representative sample of potential
      respondents

How to obtain this feedback?

It can be done either:

1. informal, open-ended interviews with several potential respondents, as if they are the research subject. The purpose of this is to determine the:
      - relevancy of the questions
      - extent to which there maybe
       problems in obtaining   responses
2. pilot testing
3. dry run
4. field trial

When is field trial necessary?
             It   is   needed   if   there   is

Basic Research Guide

substantial uncertainty in areas such as:

1) Response rate.
2) Question applicability.
3) Question performance.

Types of Question

1. **Open-Ended Questions**

   Characteristics:
   1. seems easy to write
   2. quite likely to suppress responses

   Why do some researchers use open-ended questions?

   The reason to use open – ended question is to capture unsuspected information.

   Is this reason valid?
   YES. For brief, informal questionnaires to small groups, say, ones with fewer than 50 respondents. When the group of respondents is small there can be simple listing of the responses to each question. Researchers should remember

that listing process is time-consuming and introduces error. However, open-ended questions should be avoided.

Major reason of avoidance:
-Variation in willingness and ability to respond in writing.

2. Objective Questions

These are questions where the investigator/ researcher sets the prevalent categories for the respondent to choose from.

With a few exceptions, the category "Other" should be avoided as a response option, especially when it occurs at the end of a long list of fairly lengthy choices.

Reason:
This option might be ignored by imprudent responders.

When to use *"Other (specify)."*
This should be used only when the investigator/researcher has been unable to establish the prevalent categories of response with

Basic Research Guide

reasonable certainty.

Matters to Consider in Questionnaire Development

The questions to be asked to the respondents play an important part in the research work. Researchers must have to be cautious in formulating them to be able to produce a quality output. The following matters need to be given weight : (1) Scale Point Proliferation; (2) Order of Categories; (3) Combining Categories; (4) Scale Midpoint; (5) Response Category Language and Logic;(6)Ranking Questions; (7) Unnecessary Questions; (8)Sensitive Questions; (9) Anonymity; (10) Non – returns; (11) Format and Appearance

1. Scale Point Proliferation

An example of scale point proliferation:
          1) Never
          2) Rarely
          3) Occasionally
          4) Fairly often
          5) Often
          6) Very often
      7) Almost always
      8) Always

Is scale point proliferation advisable?
No. It is risky.

Why risky?
>   - annoying, confusing to the
>   respondent, unreliable

Why unreliable?
- the very large proportion of total score
variance is due to direction of choice
rather than intensity of choice.

What scale point is sufficient?
>   - 4 to5 scale points is usually
>   quite sufficient

Why?
>   - to stimulate a reasonably reliable
>   indication of response direction.

2. Order of Categories
>   - from the lower level to the higher in left-to-
>   right order

Example:
>   1) Never
>   2) Seldom
>   3) Occasionally
>   4) Frequently

Reason:
- to avoid confusion (associating greater
response levels with lower numerals might be
confusing for some respondents)

Basic Research Guide

3. Combining Categories

Example:
1) Seldom or never
It is usually undesirable to combine categories. Combining "seldom" with "never" might be desirable if respondents would be very unlikely to mark "never" and if "seldom" would connote an almost equivalent level of activity.

4. Scale Midpoint Responses

Example of responses having midpoint:
A.
1) Agree
2) Tend to agree
3) Undecided
4) Tend to disagree
5) Disagree

B.
1) Much below average
2) Below average
3) Average
4) Above average
5) Much above average

Association of scale values 1 through 5 to these categories makes the researcher in these categories unable to reach a good result. It can yield highly misleading results. There is no assurance that a subject choosing the middle scale position harbors a neutral opinion.

What might be the reason why a respondent choose a midpoint scale?

Maybe it is a result from respondents:

> **Ignorance** - has no basis for judgment

> **Uncooperativeness** - does not want to go to the trouble of formulating an opinion.

> **Reading difficulty**- may choose "Undecided" to cover up inability to read

> **Reluctance to answer**- may wish to avoid displaying his/her true opinion

> **Inapplicability** - the question is not applicable to him

What are the strategies that may alleviate the above problem?

1) **Encourage omission of a response** when a decision cannot be reached.

2) **Choose word responses** so that a firm stand may be avoided, e.g., "tend to disagree."

Basic Research Guide

3) **Help respondents** with reading or
   interpretation of the problems.

4) **Include options explaining inability to
respond**, such as "not applicable," "no basis for
judgment," "prefer not to answer."
   In all the above cases, the researcher's best
   hope is that the respondent will not respond
   at all.

Exception where neutral position/category is required.

Examples   are:
   How much time do you spend on this job
   now?
        1) Less than before
        2) About the same
        3) More time

   The amount of homework for this course
   was
        1) too little
        2) reasonable
        3) too great

   It   would   be   unrealistic   to   expect   a
respondent   to   judge   generally   comparable
circumstances.

5. Response Category Language and Logic

The degree to which respondents concur with an declaration can be surveyed enough as a rule by the choices:
1) Agree
2) Disagree

However, when many respondents have opinions that are not very strong the below choices are better:
1) Agree
2) Tend to agree
3) Tend to disagree
4) Disagree

These options have the advantage of allowing the expression of some uncertainty.

The following options would be undesirable in most cases:

1) Strongly agree
2) Agree
3) Disagree
4) Strongly Disagree

Why undesirable?
Reason: It is objectionable. "Agree" is a very strong word. Some would say that "Strongly agree" is redundant or at best a colloquialism.

In addition, there is no comfortable resting place

for those with some uncertainty. There is no need to unsettle a segment of respondents by this or other cavalier usage of language. Another problem can arise when a number of questions all use the same response categories.

What is that problem?
- Disposal rather than return of a questionnaire due to inappropriate response categories and nonparallel stimuli.

6. Ranking Questions
Asking respondents to rank stimuli has drawbacks and should be avoided if possible. Respondents cannot be reasonably expected to rank more than six things at a single period. This must be

avoided to get away from misinterpretation of the path in their responses.

To help alleviate this latter problem, ranking questions may be framed as follows:
Example : Following are three colors for office walls:
1) Beige
2) Ivory
3) Light green
Which color do you like best? _____
Which color do you like second best? _____
Which color do you like least? _____

7. Unnecessary Questions
- may lengthen the questionnaire

- pry almost frivolously into personal matters which are often overlooked

Asking the respondents to repeat information is not only burdensome but may introduce error, especially when reporting the truth has a negative connotation.

A question might be included to check on the representativeness of the sample.
Example:
> Age: 1) below 18
> 2) 18-19
> 3) 20-21
> 4) over 21

Suggestion to this kind of question to make it valid could be by generalization like :
> 1) older
> 2) younger

8. Sensitive Questions
> - must not appear early

Reason: respondents maybe too affected

Results: will not continue; not return the questionnaire

Example of sensitive questions:
> - personal or confidential information

Where to place sensitive questions?
> - at the end of the questionnaire

Basic Research Guide

9. Anonymity

For many if not most questionnaires, it is necessary or desirable to identify respondents.

What are the common reasons?
- to check on non- returns and
- to permit associating responses with other data on the subjects.

What does the researcher promise to the respondents after stating that their responses cannot be identified?
- security of confidentiality

After stating that responses are anonymous, it is not correct to code response sheets surreptitiously or secretly to identify respondents. It is a clear violation of ethics. If a questionnaire contains sensitive questions yet must be identified for accomplishment of its purpose the best policy is to promise confidentiality but not anonymity.

What should the researcher do to have confidentiality but not anonymity?
- clearly visible code number
- respondents should be informed

10. Non- returns
- mailed questionnaire seems likely to suffer non-return

What kind of questionnaire more likely to suffer non-return?
- difficult and lengthy

Remedy?
-   usual follow-up procedures

11. Format and Appearance / Extrinsic Characteristics of Questionnaires

What should researcher take into consideration?

Researchers should consider that by the quality of what they produce:
- they are representing themselves and
- of their parent organizations

How should a questionnaire look like?
Research or survey questionnaires should:
- appear to be attractive, clearly printed and well laid out
- have slight reduction in type size and printed on both sides of good quality paper. It may reduce a carelessly arranged five pages to single sheet of paper.
- have a stamped or postpaid return envelope to be highly desirable for mailing and return address should be prominently featured on the questionnaire itself (Frary, 2007).

Basic Research Guide

Signal Phrases

Hacker (7th ed), said that signal phrase is a passage which indicates that the researcher is now displaying another point of discussion. These generally include the speaker/author's name and some justification for using him or her as an expert in this context; it may also help establish the context for the quotation" (p. 603).

Note: The examples of signal phrases below are taken from Hacker (7th ed). Some arrangements are modified to commit to memory with expediency.

In the words of researchers Redelmeier and Tibshirani, "…"

As Matt Sundeen has noted, "…"

Patti Pena, mother of a child killed by a driver distracted by a cell phone, points out that "…"

"…" writes Christine Haughney, "…"

"…" claims wireless spokesperson Annette Jacobs.

Radio hosts Tom and Ray Magliozzi offer a persuasive counterargument: "…"

Hacker (7th ed) listed some examples of

verbs in signal phrases like Acknowledge; Add; Admit ; Address; Confirm; Contend; Declare; Deny; Dispute; Emphasize; Endorse; Grant; Illustrate; Imply; Insist; Note; Observe; Point out; Reason; Refute; Reject; Report; Respond; Suggest; Think; Write, (p. 603).

Note: The topics below are pattern from an online publication written by David Neyhart and Erin Karper (n.d.). Arrangement is simplified by the compiler to make it easier for the researchers to understand   and   apply.

Basic Citation Format for Most Common Sources

Ethics governs that credit must be given to the authors or the sources of the information used in the paper except the following: familiar proverbs; well-known quotations; and common knowledge. In the text citations, APA (American Psychological Association) style requires researchers to use the past tense or present perfect tense when using signal phrases to describe earlier research.

Example: Coning (2018) found   or

          Coning (2018) has found ...

The author-date method is followed when using APA in text citation.

Basic Research Guide

Example: (Coning, 2018),

Observed that in the above given examples, it is the author's last name that should appear first followed by the year of publication. Always remember that the complete reference should appear in the reference list section at the end of the paper.

Short Quotations

Rule: a signal phrase which includes the author, year of publication, will be written before the start of the quoted words, and at the end of the quotation the page number for the reference (preceded by "p.") will be written.

Example:

According to Coning (2018), " In conducting research, researchers must be cautious " (p. 120). or

Coning (2018) found that "in conducting research, researchers must be cautious" (p. 120).

If the author is not named in a signal phrase, place the author's last name, the year of publication, and the page number in parentheses after the quotation. For example:

She stated, "in conducting research, researchers must be cautious," (Coning, 2018, p. 120), but she did not offer an explanation as to why.

Long Quotations

Rules: The following are to be noted when using a long quotation:

1. Place direct quotations longer than 40 words in a free-standing block of typewritten lines.

2. Omit quotation marks.

3. Start the quotation on a new line, indented five spaces from the left margin.

4. Type the entire quotation on the new margin, and indent the first line of any subsequent paragraph within the quotation five spaces from the new margin.

   5. Maintain double-spacing throughout. The page number for the reference (preceded by "p.") will be written after closing punctuation mark.

Example:

Coning (2018) study found the following:

In conducting a research study, the administration of questionnaire and retrieval of the same is a means of gathering the data; nevertheless, visibility and availability of the respondents found to be very difficult for the student-researchers. To approach unfamiliar respondents   and convince them to answer the survey questionnaire could be very hard for the student – researchers. (p.120)

Summary or Paraphrase

In paraphrasing an idea from another's work, the researchers have to make reference to the author

and year of publication in the   parenthetical citation, the page number for the reference (preceded by "p.") is encouraged but not required.

Example:

According to Coning (2018), students must be conscientious and need to work in the library for a certain number of hours each week.
or

Students must be conscientious and need to work in the library for a certain number of hours each week (Coning, 2018, p. 120).

Citing an Author or Authors

Two Authors

Rule:

1. Name both authors in the signal phrase,

followed by the year of publication in parentheses. Use the word "and" between the authors' names within the text each time the work is cited.

Example:
Research by Coning and Fuertes (2017) showed . . . or

2. Name both authors in the parentheses and use (&) in the parentheses.

Example: (Coning & Fuertes, 2017) . . .

Three to Five Authors
Rule:
1. List all the authors in the signal phrase or in parentheses the first time you cite the source.

Example: (Coning, Fuertes, Sonia, Betty, & Ronn, 2015) . . .

2. In subsequent citations, only use the first author's last name followed by "et al." in the signal phrase or in parentheses.
Example: (Coning et al., 2015)

(Remember in writing et al, the period should be after   al   just like the above shown example)

Six or More Authors

Rule :
1. Use the first author's name followed by et al.

Basic Research Guide

in the signal phrase or in parentheses.

Example: Conning et al. (2011) argued...

(Coning et al., 2011)

Unknown Author

Rule:
1. Cite the source by its title in the signal phrase or use the first word or two in the parentheses.

Example:
According to the study entitled Leadership Style, (2006), . . .

or

2. use the first word or two in the parentheses

Example:

An effective leader recognizes his or her personality and how operational factors or daily tasks affect his or her relationship with others ("Leadership Style," 2006).

Remember:
1. Titles of books and reports are italicized or underlined; titles of articles and chapters are in quotation marks.
2. in rare case "Anonymous" is used for the author, consider it as the author's name (Anonymous,

2001). In the reference list section, use the name Anonymous as the author.

Organization or a Government Agency as an Author

Rule:
1. Mention the organization in the signal phrase or in the parenthetical citation the first time you cite the source.

Example: According to the American Psychological Association (2000)...

2. If the organization has a well-known abbreviation, include the abbreviation in brackets the first time the source is cited and then use only the abbreviation in later citations.

Example:

First citation: (Community Health Workers [CHW], 2015)

Second citation: (CHW, 2015)

Two or More Works in the Same Parentheses

Rule: When your parenthetical citation includes two or more works, order them the same way they appear in the reference list, separated by a semi-colon.

Basic Research Guide

Example: (Jehan, 2013; Jerriot, 2009)

Authors with the Same Last Name

Rule: To avoid confusion, use first initials with the last names.

Example: (J. Anon, 2011; T. Anon, 2009)

Two or More Works by the Same Author in the Same Year

Rule: If you have two sources by the same author in the same year, use lower-case letters (a, b, c) with the year to order the entries in the reference list. Use the lower-case letters with the year in the parenthetical citation.

Example: Research by Jerriot (2003a) illustrated that...

Personal Communication

Rule: 1. For interviews, letters, e-mails, and other person-to-person communication, cite the **communicator's name**, and the date of the communication.

Example: (E. Riols, personal communication, March 9, 2009).

E. Riols also claimed that lack of self-regulatory skills appears to be a potential identification for students to fail from their class activities, (personal communication, February 5, 2009).

2. Do not include personal communication in the reference list section.

Citing Indirect Sources
Rule:
1. If you use a source that was cited in another source, name the original source in your signal phrase and include the secondary source in the parentheses.

Example: Thomas argued that... (as cited in Smatha, 2003, p. 102).

2. List the secondary source in your reference list section.

Electronic Sources

Rule: If possible, cite an electronic document the same as any other document by using the author-date style.

Example: Roger (2000) explained...

Unknown Author and Unknown Date

Rule: Use the title in your signal phrase or the first word or two of the title in the parentheses

Basic Research Guide

and use the abbreviation "n.d." (for "no date").

Example:

> Another study about students'
> learning skills demonstrated that, to provide
> appropriate learning environments and valid
> assessment instruments to monitor students'
> ability to self-regulate, are not easy tasks
> ("Self-regulatory Skills," n.d.).

Sources without Page Numbers

Rule: Try to include information that will
help readers find the passage being cited. When an
electronic document has numbered paragraphs, use
the ¶ symbol, or the abbreviation "para." followed by
the paragraph number (Hall, 2001, ¶ 5) or (Hall,
2001, para. 5).

If the paragraphs are not numbered and the
document includes headings, provide the appropriate
heading and specify the paragraph under that
heading. Note that in some electronic sources, like
Web pages, people can use the Find function in their
browser to locate any passages you cite.

Example:

According to Samantha (1995), ... (Miles and
Miles Away section, para. 6).

Remember: Never use the page numbers of Web

pages you print out; different computers print Web pages with different pagination.

Sources that Need Quotations

These are: journal articles, articles from edited collections, television series episodes, and song titles. Quotation marks are placed around the

titles of these shorter works.

Example:

(1)."Minute Talk: Understanding the Words";

(2)."The Only Woman."

Note: The discussion below is taken from the article of Key (1997). Since this subject matter is crucial in the making of a research paper the compiler opted not to alter any word in this topic.

Sampling Methods

According to the online article of Key (1997), there are six sampling methods. These methods are:

1. Randomization. Random sampling as suggested by Van Dalen (1979) often means chance or a haphazard method of assignment to many people, but in reality it is a carefully controlled

Basic Research Guide

process. Randomization is used to eliminate bias, both conscious and unconscious, that researchers might introduce while selecting a sample. Kerlinger (1986) described randomization as the assignment of objects (subjects, treatments, groups, etc.) of a population to subsets (sample) of the population in such a way that, for any given assignment to a subset (sample), every member of the population has an equal probability of being chosen for that assignment. Randomization is essential for probability samples which are the only samples that can generalize results back to the population. Kerlinger (1986) reported that random sampling is important because it is required by inferential statistics. If the researcher desires to make inferences about populations based on the behavior of samples, then random sampling must be used.

2. Stratification. Stratified sampling is a procedure for selecting a sample that includes identified subgroups from the population in the proportion that they exist in the population. This method can be used to select equal numbers from each of the identified subgroups if comparisons between subgroups is important. A good example of stratified sampling would be to divide the population into men and women. The different strata to use for each study would be determined in part by the review of literature of previous research. The purpose of stratified sampling is to guarantee the desired distribution among the selected subgroups of the population.

3. Proportional. Proportional sampling (Van Dalen, 1979) provides the researcher a way to achieve even greater representativeness in the sample of the population. This is accomplished by selecting individuals at random from the subgroup in proportion to the actual size of the group in the total

population. Proportional sampling is used in combination with stratified and cluster sampling.

4. Clusters. The most used method in educational research according to Kerlinger (1986) is cluster sampling. Groups of elements (clusters) instead of individuals from the population are used for the sample. Cluster sampling often is more convenient when the population is very large. Often is not possible to randomly select from the entire population but is more manageable when using clusters because of time, expense, and convenience. A cluster sampling is using schools as clusters and randomly selecting from the list of schools instead of randomly selecting individuals from a list that includes all schools. This can help the researcher cut down on travel expense, time, etc. One problem with cluster sampling is that it usually produces a larger sampling error than a simple random sample of the same size because the clusters tend to be more similar within the cluster, reducing the representativeness of the sample (Van Dalen, 1979).

5. Systematic. In some cases when the

Basic Research Guide

population of a study is available as a list, a sample is drawn from certain intervals on the list. The starting point is randomly chosen and then in every so many numbers another individual is chosen from the list and added to the sample. This method can be equal to random selection only if the names were randomized at the beginning. Van Dalen (1979)

cautions researcher to be wary of departure from randomness of the list because of structure, some trends, or cyclical fluctuation.

6. Purposive. Kerlinger (1986) explained purposive sampling as another type of non-probability sampling, which is characterized by the use of judgment and a deliberate effort to obtain representative samples by including typical areas or groups in the sample. In other words, the researcher attempts to do what proportional clustering with randomization accomplishes by using human judgment and logic. As a result, there are many opportunities for error. In addition, non-probability samples do not use random sampling which makes them unacceptable for generalizing back to the population.

In random sampling each object has an equal and independent opportunity of being chosen. Stratified sampling involves the identification of the variable and subgroups (strata) for which you want to guarantee appropriate representation (either proportional or equal). To use cluster sampling, you must list and identify all clusters that comprise the population and estimate the average number of population members per cluster to determine the number of clusters needed for the sample. Proportional sampling determines the ratio of individuals in subgroups for which you want proportional representation. Once the strata, cluster, or ratio has been determined, individual objects, clusters, or individuals in a subgroup are randomly selected. Systematic sampling takes every nth name (n=size of population divided by desired sample size) on a list of the population until the desired sample size is reached.

Note: The discussion below is taken from the article of Key (1997). Since this subject matter is crucial in the making of research the compiler opted not to alter any word in this topic.

Determination of Sample Size

The first thing that is needed is to identify or define the population. Jaccard (1983) defined population as the aggregate of all cases to which one wishes to generalize. At this time, it is necessary to determine if your research requires the identification of subgroups and if so define the subgroups within the population. To have a sample that is of use it needs to be as close as possible to being representative of the complete population. Popham & Sirotnik (1973) contend that in order to draw legitimate inferences about populations from samples that the sample has to be a representative of the population and randomly selected.

Van Dalen (1979) lists three factors that he considers to determine the size of an adequate sample as (1) the nature of the population, (2) the type of investigation, and (3) the degree of precision desired. The formula for estimating the sample size and a table for determining the sample size based on confidence level needed from a given population were provided by Krejcie & Morgan (1970).

$$S = \frac{X^2 \, NP \, (1-P)}{d^2 \, (N-1) + X^2 P \, (1-P)} \text{ where}$$

S = required sample size; N = the given population size ; P = population proportion that for table construction has been assumed to be .50, as this magnitude yields the maximum possible sample size required d = the degree of accuracy as reflected by the amount of error that can be tolerated in the fluctuation of a sample proportion p about the population proportion P - the value for d being .05 in the calculations for entries in the table, a quantity equal to

$$\pm 1.96 \, \sigma_p$$

X^2 = table value of chi square for one degree of freedom relative to the desired level of confidence, which was 3.841 for the .95 confidence level represented by entries in the table.

TABLE FOR DETERMINING NEEDED SIZE *S* OF A RANDOMLY CHOSEN SAMPLE FROM A GIVEN FINITE POPULATION OF *N* CASES SUCH THAT THE SAMPLE PROPORTION *p* WILL BE WITHIN ± .05 OF THE POPULATION PROPORTION *P* WITH A 95 PERCENT LEVEL OF CONFIDENCE.

Population Size	Sample Size	Population Size	Sample Size	Population Size	Sample Size
10	10	220	140	1200	291
15	14	230	144	1300	297
20	19	240	148	1400	302
25	24	250	152	1500	306
30	28	260	155	1600	310
35	32	270	159	1700	313
40	36	280	162	1800	317

Basic Research Guide

45	40	290	165	1900	320
50	44	300	169	2000	322
55	48	320	175	2200	327
60	52	340	181	2400	331
65	56	360	186	2600	335
70	59	380	191	2800	338
75	63	400	196	3000	341
80	66	420	201	3500	346
85	70	440	205	4000	351
90	73	460	210	4500	354
95	76	480	214	5000	357
100	80	500	217	6000	361
110	86	550	226	7000	364

120	92	600	234	8000	367
130	97	650	242	9000	368
140	103	700	248	10000	370
150	108	750	254	15000	375
160	113	800	260	20000	377
170	118	850	265	30000	379
180	123	900	269	40000	380
190	127	950	274	50000	381
200	132	1000	278	75000	382
210	136	1100	285	100000	384

Note: The table above presented the representative sample of the projected potential respondents as illustrated by Key (1997) in his article.

Note further: To avoid erroneous interpretation of the succeeding topics namely: Statistics and Scale of Measurement the compiler preferred not to alter any word used by the author of these

articles.

Statistics

In every research, statistical analysis is present. It is an element of the research methodology. According to Heffner, (2004), "A statistic is a numerical representation of information." The act of counting, measuring, calculating, computing or putting a figure to sort out information is quantifying. When we are quantifying we are utilizing statistical methods. Heffner further explained that, "There are two major branches of statistics, each with specific goals and specific formulas. These are the descriptive statistics and the inferential statistics. To use inferential statistics, only a sample of the population is needed. Descriptive statistics, however, require the entire population be used" (2004).

Statistics gives the impression of a difficult task. Statisticians are equipped with substantial knowledge to be of assistance to researchers to lay down considerable information gathered from their tedious work.

Scales of Measurement

According to Dr. Christopher L. Heffner, the author, statistical information, including numbers and sets of numbers, has specific qualities that are of interest to researchers. These qualities, including magnitude, equal intervals, and absolute zero, determine what scale of measurement is being used and therefore what statistical procedures are best.

Magnitude refers to the ability to know if one score is greater than, equal to, or less than another score. Equal intervals mean that the possible scores are each an equal distance from each other. And finally, absolute zero refers to a point where none of the scale exists or where a score of zero can be assigned.

When these three scale qualities are combined, there are four scales of measurement that can be determined. The lowest level is the nominal scale, which represents only names and therefore has none of the three qualities. A list of students in alphabetical order, a list of favorite cartoon characters, or the names on an organizational chart would all be classified as nominal data. The second level, called ordinal data, has magnitude only, and can be looked at as any set of data that can be placed in order from greatest to lowest but where there is no absolute zero and no equal intervals. Examples of this type of scale would include Likert Scales and the Thurstone Technique.

The third type of scale is called an interval scale, and possesses both magnitude and equal intervals, but no absolute zero. Temperature is a classic example of an interval scale because each degree is the same distance apart and it is easy to tell if one temperature is greater than, equal to, or less than another. Temperature; however, has no absolute zero because there is (theoretically) no point

Basic Research Guide

where temperature does not exist.

Finally, the fourth and highest scale of measurement is called a ratio scale. A ratio scale contains all three qualities and is often the scale that statisticians prefer because the data can be more easily analyzed. Age, height, weight, and scores on a 100-point test would all be examples of ratio scales. If you are 20 years old, you not only know that you are older than someone who is 15 years old (magnitude) but you also know that you are five years' older (equal intervals). With a ratio scale, it also has a point where none of the scale exists; when a person is born his or her age is zero. The table below simplified the above topic, (2004).

Scale Level	Scale of Measurement	Scale Qualities	Example(s)
4	Ratio	Magnitude Equal Intervals Absolute Zero	Age, Height, Weight, Percentage
3	Interval	Magnitude Equal Intervals	Temperature
2	Ordinal	Magnitude	Likert Scale, Anything rank

			ordered
1	Nominal	None	Names, Lists of words

The table above simplified the topic.

BASIC GUIDE III

Listing of Sources

The different disciplines have different citation formats, however in social sciences the researchers are required to use APA (American Psychological Association) format. All other humanities departments use the MLA (Modern Language Association) style in their references. The differences are only in the method of citing a text, not in quoting it ("Writing Policy", 2009).

In an online article it was mentioned that, the information that is written or added to the research work should come from the thoughts and ideas of the researcher himself/ herself if not then the author of the information and the website should be given credit to avoid plagiarism.

Plagiarism is defined as an illegal use of other people's idea; introduce and consider this idea as his own. Considering the word illegal, this means that the use of others idea is without permission (Alianess, 2011). And thus, this makes this work as a plagiarized one and that should be avoided to produce a quality research output.

Using other people's work is referred to as plagiarism. This means that the writer has: (1) "only changed around a few words and phrases, or changed the order of the original's sentences, (2) failed to cite a source for any of the ideas or facts" ("Plagiarism", 2004). To avoid being charge for plagiarism one should construct what he understands from other people's work using his own words AND cite the origin or the source of his ideas.

Here are helpful ways to avoid plagiarism:

1. Paraphrase. Write the idea or opinion in your own words accurately from the original. Rearranging or replacing few words is not paraphrasing.

2. Correct quotation. When the use of the phrases or sentences of the other people cannot be avoided it must be placed within quotation marks.

3. Proper Source citation. The source of the facts or ideas MUST be cited.

The researchers do not need to give credit to generally known information. They are facts that can be found anywhere and most likely known by many people. These are: (1) familiar proverbs, (2) well-known quotations, and (3) common knowledge ("What is Plagiarism", 1995).

Citing Sources of Work

There are two parts of citations. These are citations that can be found: (1) within the text of the

Basic Research Guide

paper, and (2) in the reference page. In the two popular styles of citations namely APA (American Psychological Association) and MLA (Modern Language Association) the terms in-text citation and parenthetical citation are interchangeably used. The lists of sources that researchers used in writing their papers are known in different names although they suggest the same meaning. In APA it is called as the Reference page while in MLA it is called as the Works Cited page ("Two Elements", n.d.).

In citing sources of work (within the text) using APA style few strategies are to be remembered: (1) Parentheses ( ) are to be used always around the citation of the information. The citation consists of the author's last name, the year the work was published, and the pages that are being referenced; (2) In making direct quotes, the author's last name, the year the work was published, and the pages that are being referenced should be included together at the end of the quote; (3) When paraphrasing, the author's last name, the year the work was published, and the pages that are being referenced are to be included at the end of the sentence; (4) When the information cited has two authors, use an ampersand (&) between their surnames; when there are more than two authors use an ampersand (&) between the last two surnames ("Parenthetical Citations", 2007).

Some Standards in Writing References

Page

The References page should be written on a separate page and be placed at the end of the research paper. The title **References** should be centered at the top of the page. The entire references page should be double-spaced. If one of the entries is longer than one line, the second line should be indented one-half inch from the left margin. This is called hanging indention. The entries should be arranged in alphabetical order (using the author's last name). The authors should be written with their last name followed by their first initial ("How to Cite APA Format", n.d.) Italicize titles of longer works such as books and journals. When referring to any work that is NOT a journal, such as a book, article, or Web page, capitalize only the first letter of the first word of a title and subtitle, the first word after a colon or a dash in the title, and proper nouns. Do not capitalize the first letter of the second word in a hyphenated compound word. Capitalize all major words in journal titles (Neyhart, Karper & Seas, n.d.).

Reference Page Format

Note: The patterns of the selected format and examples discussed below on how to list sources in the reference page section are taken from the online article written by Neyhart, Karper & Seas (n.d.)

They are compiled and arranged in a simple

Basic Research Guide

way so that students who are new to research work would be able to apply correctly what they learned and find them easy to remember while in the process of making their academic papers.

A. Format by Author/Authors

1) Single Author (regardless of the type of work (book, article, electronic resource, etc.)

Rule: Last name first, followed by author initials.

Example:

> Berndt, T. J. (2002). Friendship quality and social development. *Current Directions in Psychological Science, 11*, 7-10.

2) Two Authors

Rule: List by their last names and initials. Use the "&" instead of "and."

Example:

> Wegener, D. T., & Petty, R. E. (1994). Mood management across affective states: The hedonic contingency hypothesis. *Journal of Personality & Social Psychology, 66*, 1034-1048.

3) Three to Six Authors

Rule: List by last names and initials; commas separate author names, while the last author name is preceded again by "&"

Example:

> Kernis, M. H., Cornell, D. P., Sun, C. R., Berry, A., & Harlow, T. (1993). There's more to self-esteem than   whether it is high or low: The importance of stability of self-esteem. *Journal of Personality and Social Psychology, 65*, 1190-1204.

4) More Than Six Authors

Rule: If there are more than six authors, list the first six as above and then "et al.," which stands for "and others." Place a period after "et al." not after "et".

Example:

> Harris, M., Karper, E., Stacks, G., Hoffman, D., DeNiro, R., Cruz, P., et al. (2001). Writing labs and the Hollywood connection. *Journal of Film and Writing, 44*(3), 213-245.

5) Organization as Author

Example:

> American Psychological Association.

Basic Research Guide

(2003).

6) Unknown Author

Rule: Use a shortened version of the source's title instead of an author's name. Use quotation marks and italics as appropriate.

Example 1:

Merriam-Webster's collegiate dictionary (10thed.).(1993).Springfield,MA: Merriam-Webster.

Example 2: Two sources would appear as follows:

(*Merriam-Webster's*, 1993) and ("New Drug," 1993).

7) Two or More Works by the Same Author

Rule: Use the author's name for all entries and list the entries by the year (earliest comes first).

Example:

Berndt, T.J. (1981).

Berndt, T.J. (1999).

8) Two or More Works by the Same Author in the Same Year

Rule: Organize them in the reference list alphabetically by the title of the article or chapter. Then assign letter suffixes to the year. Refer to these sources in your essay as they appear in your reference list, e.g.: "Berdnt (1981a) makes similar claims..."

Example:

Berndt, T. J. (1981a). Age changes and changes over time in prosocial intentions and behavior between friends. *Developmental Psychology, 17,* 408-416.

Berndt, T. J. (1981b). Effects of friendship on pro-social intentions and behavior.*Child Development,52,*636-643

B. Articles in Periodicals

APA style dictates that authors are named last name followed by initials; publication year goes between parentheses, followed by a period. The title of the article is in sentence-case, meaning only the first word and proper nouns in the title are capitalized. The periodical title is run in title case, and is followed by the volume number which, with the title, is also italicized or underlined.

Example:
Author, A. A., Author, B. B., & Author, C.

Basic Research Guide

C. (Year). Title of article. *Title of Periodical, volume number* (issue number), pages.

C. Article in Journal Paginated by Volume.

Journals that are paginated by volume begin with page one in issue one, and continue numbering issue two where issue one ended, etc.

Example:

> Harlow, H. F. (1983). Fundamentals for preparing psychology journal articles. *Journal of Comparative and Physiological Psychology, 55*, 893-896.

D. Article in Journal Paginated by Issue.

Journals paginated by issue begin with page one every issue; therefore, the issue number gets indicated in parentheses after the volume. The parentheses and issue number are not italicized or underlined.

Example:
> Scruton, R. (1996). The eclipse of listening. *The New Criterion, 15* (30), 5-13.

E. Article in a Magazine

Example:

Henry, W. A., III. (1990, April 9). Making the grade in today's schools. *Time, 135*, 28-31.

F. Article in a Newspaper.

Unlike other periodicals, p. or pp. precedes page numbers for a newspaper reference in APA style. Single pages take p., e.g., p. B2; multiple pages take pp., e.g., pp. B2, B4 or pp. C1, C3-C4.

Example:

Schultz, S. (2005, December 28). Calls made to strengthen state energy policies. *The Country Today*, pp.1A, 2A.

G. Format for Books
Note: **For "Location," you should always list the city, but you should also include the state if the city is unfamiliar or if the city could be confused with one in another state.**

Example:

Calfee, R. C., & Valencia, R. R. (1991). *APA guide to preparing manuscripts for journal publication.*Washington, DC: American Psychological Association.

Basic Research Guide

H. Edited Book, No Author

Example:

> Duncan,G.J.,& Brooks-Gunn, J.(Eds.).
> (1997).*Consequences of growing up
> poor*. New York: Russell Sage
> Foundation.

I. Edited Book with an Author or Authors
Example:

> Plath, S. (2000). *The unabridged
> journals* (K.V. Kukil, Ed.). New York:
> Anchor.

J. An Entry in an Encyclopedia

Example:

> Bergmann, P. G. (1993).   Relativity.
> In *The new encyclopedia britannica*
> (Vol.   26,   pp.501-508).*Chicago:
> Encyclopedia Britannica.*

K. Work Discussed in a Secondary Source
Rule: List the source the work was discussed in:

Example:

Coltheart, M., Curtis, B., Atkins, P., & Haller, M. (1993). Models of reading aloud: Dual-route and parallel-distributed-processing approaches. *Psychological Review, 100*, 589-608.

Remember: Give the secondary source in the references list; in the text, name the original work, and give a citation for the secondary source.

For example, if Seidenberg and McClelland's work is cited in Coltheart et al. and you did not read the original work, list the Coltheart et al. reference in the References. In the text, use the following citation:

Example:

In Seidenberg and McClelland's study (as cited in Coltheart, Curtis, Atkins, & Haller, 1993), ...

L. Dissertation Abstract

Example:

Yoshida, Y. (2001). Essays in urban transportation (Doctoral dissertation,Boston College,2001). *Dissertation Abstracts International, 62*, 7741A.

Basic Research Guide

M. Government Document

Example:
National Institute of Mental Health. (1990). *Clinical training in serious mental illness* (DHHS Publication No. ADM 90-1679). Washington, DC:U.S. Government Printing Office.

N. Report from a Private Organization

Example:
American Psychiatric Association. (2000). *Practice guidelines for the treatment of patients with eating disorders (*2nd ed.). Washington, D.C.: Author.

O. Format for Electronic Sources

1. Article from an Online Periodical

Rule: Online articles follow the same guidelines for printed articles. Include all information the online host makes available, including an issue number in parentheses.

Example:
Author, A. A., & Author, B. B. (Date of publication). Title of article. *Title of Online Periodical, volume number*

*(*issue number if available). Retrieved month day, year, from http://www. someaddress.com/full/ url/

Bernstein, M. (2002). 10 tips on writing the living Web. *A List   Apart: For People Who Make Websites, 149.* retrieved May 2, 2006, from http://www.alistapart.com/ articles/writeliving

2. Online Scholarly Journal Article

Example:
Author, A. A., & Author, B. B. (Date of publication). Title of article. *Title of Journal, volume number.* retrieved month day, year, from http://www.some address.com/full/url/

Kenneth, I. A. (2000). A Buddhist response to the   nature of human rights. *Journal of Buddhist Ethic8.*retrieved February 20, 2001, from http://www.cac.psu.edu /jbe/twocont.html

If the article appears as a printed version as well, the URL is not required. Use   "Electronic version" in brackets after the article's title.

Whitmeyer, J.M. (2000).Power through appointment [Electronic version].

Basic Research Guide

Social Science Research, 29, 535-555.

3. Article from a Database

When referencing material obtained from an online database (such as a database in the library), provide appropriate print citation information (formatted just like a "normal" print citation would be for that type of work). Then add information that gives the date of retrieval and the proper name of the database. This will allow people to retrieve the print version if they do not have access to the database from which you retrieved the article. You can also include the item number or accession number in parentheses at the end, but the APA manual says that this is not required.

Example:
> Smyth, A. M., Parker, A. L., & Pease, D. L. (2002). A study of enjoyment of peas. *Journal of Abnormal Eating, 8*(3). retrieved February 20, 2003, from PsycARTICLES database.

4. E-mail

> E-mails are not included in the list of references, though you parenthetically cite them in your main text:

Example:

> (E.Robbins, personal communication, January 4, 2001).

To further researchers' knowledge on how to write the sources in the references another web article entitled, "How to Cite APA Format," (n.d.) enumerated some items that should be included in each entry in the references:

- The author(s) or editor(s) - with surname first
- The date of publication
- The complete title of the work (italicized)
- The edition (if applicable)
- The publication title (for articles and periodicals only)
- The volume number (for articles and periodicals only)
- The specific pages referenced (if applicable)
- The place where it was published (for books)
- The publisher (for books)

Bibliography should include only items discussed in the text and if other things which have been read but not cited in the text, a separate section be added with the heading "Additional Reading" (" Two Elements in Citing Your Work," n.d.), however; according to Andres & Andres (1996) " bibliography includes all materials consulted whether or not they are mentioned in the text while references include only all those materials actually cited in the text.

Abstract

Purposely, an abstract will aid the readers. It

Basic Research Guide

will give them the idea about the content of the academic study or an article. It is necessary to know how to write an abstract since this is the way to help the readers to understand easily the problem or topic of concentration in the study.

What are to be included in the abstract?

Basically, the proper sequence in writing an abstract includes: (1) topic, (2) research question, (3) methods, (4) results, and (5) conclusion ("How Do I Write an Abstract?" n.d.). This means to say that researchers should have to read intelligently, follow the steps, and note carefully the content of the study.

As illustrated   in an online article entitled "How Do I Write an Abstract?" this is how it is to be presented observing strictly the APA pattern:

Begin a new page. Include a page header in the upper right-hand of every page. To create a page header, type the first 2-3 words of the title of the paper, insert five spaces, then give the page number. On the first line of the abstract page, center the word "Abstract" (otherwise unformatted, no bold, italics, underlining, or quotation marks).Beginning with the next line, write a concise summary of the key points of your research. (Do not indent.) The abstract should be a single paragraph double-spaced of less than 120 words (n.d.).

Two to three hundred (200 – 300) words for

abstract is good as well ("Writing Scientific Abstract", 1995).

Sample Abstract

ABSTRACT

This study was conducted to investigate the most difficult item student-researchers of Political Science 8 in La Salle University encountered when they conducted their research study during the first semester of the school year 2008-2009. The descriptive survey method was utilized in this study. The researcher – made instruments consisted of open - ended questions were administered to the 14 students officially enrolled in subject Political Science 8. The study showed that the cooperation of respondents outside the academic institution was a very crucial problem for student researchers. To some extent, students felt that personal problems like time and stress management disturbed their concentration. 66% of the respondents found it difficult to finish their research.

References

Andres, T. D., & Andres, P. I. (1996). Thesis. *How to make all kinds of assignments and homeworks. Chapter 14. p84.* Our Lady of Manaoag Publisher.

Basic Research Guide

Alianess. (2011). Plagiarism, what is and how to avoid it. retrieved December 20, 2007, from http://amarpals.com/?p=5400

APA documentation, The writer's handbook. (2009). UW Madison writing Center. retrieved March 17, 2011, from http://writing.wisc.edu /Handbook/ReviewofLiterature.html

Estolas, J. V., & Boquirin, D. T. (1973). *Fundamentals of research*. Manila. Miranda and Sons.

Frary, R.B.(2007). A brief guide to questionnaire development. *Office of Measurement and Research Service.* Virginia Polytechnic Institute and State University. retrieved October 5, 2007, from http://www.son.wisc.edu/rdsu/library/ questionnaire.pdf

Hamid, S., & Baker, J. R. (2007). Genre and the research paper. retrieved March 25, 2009, from http://owl. english.purdue.edu/owl/ resource/658/02/

Heffner, C. L. (2004). Research methods. *PsychOnline. The Virtual Psychology Classroom.* retrieved October 11, 2008, from http://allpsych. com/researchmethods/validityreliabilty.html

How do I write an abstract?. (n.d). retrieved January 12, 2008, from http://academiaresearch. com/sign.htm

How to cite APA format. (n.d). retrieved March 22, 2009, from http://www.mahalo.com/How_to _Cite_in_APA_Format.

How to write research paper. (n.d). retrieved March 7, 2009, from http://www.essaytown.com/ writing/how-to-write- research-paper

Informal guidelines of research paper writing. (2010). Global Journals Inc. (US) retrieved: May 27, 2011, from http://www. globaljournals. org/index.php?option=com_content&view=article&i d 171&Itemid=371

Key, J. P. (1997). Sampling. *Research design in occupational Education.* Oklahoma State University. retrieved February 24, 2010, from http://www.okstate.edu/ag/agedcm4h/academic/aged 5980a/5980/newpage15.htm

Le Gates , R. (1999). Research methods. retrieved August1,2007,http://userwww.sfsu.edu/~dlegates/ur bs492/syllabus.htm

Mc Granaghan, M. (n.d.). Proposal writing. *Guidelines on writing a research proposal.* retrieved March 20, 2009, from http://www2.hawaii.edu/~matt/proposal.html

Basic Research Guide

Moore, J. (1999). How to write research paper. retrieved January 20, 2008, from http://www. essaytown.com/writing/how-to-write-research-paper

Neyhart , D., Karper, E., & Seas, K.(n.d.) APA formatting   and style   guide.   retrieved January 12, 2008, from   http://owl.english.purdue. edu/owl/resource/560/01.

 Parenthetical citations. (2007). retrieved October 25, 2010, from http://www.mahalo.com/how-to-cite/

Plagiarism: What it is and how to recognize and avoid it. (2004). *Code of   Student Rights, Responsibilities, and Conduct of Indiana University. Writing Tutorial Services, Indiana University, Bloomington, IN*. Ballantine Hall 206, 1020 E. Kirkwood Ave. Bloomington, IN 47405. Retrieved: December 20, 2007.   *from* http://www.indiana. edu/~wts/pamphlets/plagiarism.shtml.

Research methods. (2005). retrieved August 1, 2007, from   http://bss.sfsu.edu/urbs/courses.htm.

Research and writing. (n.d.). retrieved May 30, 2007, from www.researcheden.com

Salier, R. (2008). Geography/definition question. retrieved : March   17, 2011, from http://en.allexperts.com/q/Geography1729/2008/4/D efinition-question.htm

Trimmer, J. F. (1992). *Writing with a purpose*. Ball State University. Houghton Mifflin Company.
Two elements in citing your work. (n.d.). Retrieved March 7, 2009, from http://weber.ucsd.edu/~j moore/courses/researchpapers.htl

What is plagiarism. (1995). retrieved March 23, 2009, from http://kidshealth.org/kid/feeling/ school/plagiarism.html

Why and how to create a useful outline. (2007). Purdue OWL. retrieved April 16, 2009, from http://owl.english.purdue.edu/owl/ resource/544/02/

Write a literature review.(2011). *The Regents of the University of California.* University Library. Santa Cruz, CA 95064. retrieved : March 17, 2011, from http://library.ucsc.edu/help/howto/write-a-literature review.

Writing policy. (2009). retrieved March 28, 2009, from http:// academia-research.com/sign.htm.

Writing scientific abstracts.(n.d.) *Purdue University Writing Lab. Heavilon* 226. retrieved March 10, 2008, from http://owl.english.purdue.edu/

A****A**

ABOUT THE AUTHOR

 She is a holder of the degree of Bachelor of Laws at Misamis University in 1996; Master in Business Administration at Immaculate Conception College-La Salle in 2000; Doctor of Business Administration, at the University of San Jose-Recoletos, Cebu City in 2006.

In her twenty (20) years of service at La Salle University in the Philippines, she held the Subject Coordinator office of the Social Sciences Department and later, she served as the Director of Human Resource. After the end of her appointment term in the said office she functioned as the Head of the Doctor of Business Administration programme in the College of Business and Economics of the said university.

She presented a paper in the Regional Challenges to Multidisciplinary Innovation Conference in 2015 and reaped the Best Paper Award and Best Paper Presentation. The Global Illuminators in Dubai, UEA, gave these awards.

In November, 2013, she was awarded as one of the seven Outstanding Researchers of the Philippines during the Asian Conference on Multidisciplinary Research in Higher Education (ACMRHE 2013) held in Manila, Philippines. Up to this date, she is a Senior Member of International Economics Development Research Center (IEDRC) and Peer Reviewer of The Research Council of Oman (TRC).

She published her research studies in various printed and e-Journals and had attended numerous conferences which are held in the local and international level. She is an active contributor at Social Science Research Network's (SSRN)-Elsevier an elibrary and to a well-known site of the scientists and researchers called Researchgate.